Happy Travels 101

Don't leave home without these cruise, flight, safety, packing and sightseeing tips

Toni Pike

First published in May 2017 – *Kindle Edition.*

This is the first paperback edition: November 2017

ISBN 9781973299110

Happy Travels 101

Become a travel expert before you leave home.

Here are hundreds of tips that will help to enhance your journey. Find out how to select and make the most of your next cruise, how to cope with a long-haul flight and how to write a travel preparation checklist. Discover how to explore any destination, the best tips for escorted tours and the best travel booking tips. Don't miss the recommendations on travel safety, senior travel and travel photography. And get some inspiration from the travel packing guide.

There is so much to be seen all over the world: breathtaking landscapes, ancient ruins, towns steeped in history, fascinating cultures and modern marvels. Here is your chance to master the art of successful globetrotting! Don't leave home without reading it.

About the Author

Toni Pike is an Australian who loves to travel the world doing research for her thrillers. *The Jotham Fletcher Mystery Thriller Series* is available at Amazon. She enjoys sharing travel photos on her Instagram page: @authorlovestravel. You can also follower her at www.tonipike.com.

Other works

The Jotham Fletcher Mystery Thriller Series
Book 1: The Magus Covenant
Book 2: The Rock of Magus
Book 3: The Magus Epiphany

Table of Contents

Become a travel expert before you leave home

My goal in writing this book is to help you have the best possible experience on any overseas vacation. Whether you are planning your first trip abroad or have travelled many times before, here is practical advice that you can use enhance your next journey. You will be better prepared to cope with any challenges that you might face, and able to focus instead on having a wonderful time.

All the advice in here comes from my o,wn experience. Learn my packing and travel preparation secrets, read my suggestions on how to explore any destination and find out all my tips for selecting and enjoying a cruise. Discover how I cope with long-haul flights and check my recommendations on safety, travel photography and travel for seniors.

Travel is one of my passions and I have seen some amazing places around the world that I have used as settings in my novels. It is the perfect excuse to do some research!

My first overseas trip was decades ago, but I have toured extensively over the last twelve years. I have also spent time living in America and England, when my husband was posted there for work. Cruising has become one of my favourite modes of travel, and I've enjoyed both long and short cruises in many parts the world. I have also taken many escorted coach tours and travelled independently. Because I come from Australia, I've been on more long-haul flights and visited more airports than I care to remember.

Now I want to share my insights and help you to have a successful journey.

The world is an amazing place

Are there places in the world that you have always wanted to visit? People of all ages now travel far more extensively than ever before and most find it an enriching and exciting experience.

I love to travel because there is so much to seen: extraordinary landscapes, ancient ruins, cities and towns steeped in history, fascinating cultures and modern marvels. Choose to sail through the Panama Canal or the fiords of Norway. Explore the ruins of Pompeii, the Parthenon in Athens, or the Neolithic monument of Stonehenge in Britain. Visit the Vatican City in the heart of Rome, swim in the warm waters of Fiji or attend a concert at the Sydney Opera House.

Why miss out on all of that?

Travel also gives you the chance to see how everything operates in another country. I have been surprised to find some excellent transport systems, wonderful public spaces, delicious food and interesting philosophies that gave me fresh ideas and a new perspective on life. It is also exciting to meet people from other lands and discover just how much we have in common.

Travel is a modern benefit

Hundreds of years ago, our ancestors rarely ventured further than their own town or the nearby villages. Only wealthy people or sailors would travel overseas, and they would return with fantastic stories.

Now many people are able to travel, and an increasing number of us have visited a wide range of destinations. Cruise ships are sailing to the four corners of the Earth and planes are taking off every few seconds from our major airports. We really are very lucky to have so many options.

Try to take any opportunities that you have to see other parts of the world as well as your own country. Think of the enjoyment to be had in experiencing the scenery, architecture, history and culture of another land.

Travel before time runs out

My opinion is that we should all make the most of the one life that we are given. You never know what may be just around the corner, perhaps an accident or health problem that could curtail your plans for the future. Days turn into weeks and months so quickly, and soon another year has come to an end. If you are longing to travel and have the means to do so, then consider including that as one of your goals and take steps to make it a reality.

I am not advising that you quit your job, leave your family, borrow money, give up your studies or act irresponsibly and unwisely. All I am saying is that if the time is right, then consider making a start and not leaving it for another two years or five years into the future.

Jump on that train of life before it derails, and take your journey.

Read this guide – it will take you less than two hours - and master the art of successful globetrotting.

My 8 Top Travel Booking Tips

Before you set off on any overseas trip you need to make some bookings. There is nothing to stop you booking a flight and then, when you arrive at your destination, choosing accommodation on the spot and having total flexibility to decide what you want to do each day.

I have the opposite approach, preferring to have almost everything booked before my departure and selecting each item with close attention to detail. Nothing is ever foolproof and I still make mistakes but it helps me to coordinate transport, accommodation and sightseeing to make the best use of my time.

Now we come to the question of how to go about making those bookings - and that will be the first step in making your travel dreams a reality. Here are my eight top tips for the process of booking the key elements of your trip. Those are the flights, tours, cruises, accommodation and any form of transport.

Tip 1: Decide on your budget and style of travel

The most important aspects to consider before you plan any trip are your budget and personal preferences. Everybody will have different interests and goals for their travel, and you also need to consider your age, health and physical capabilities. Some people will be looking for an adventurous vacation, and might be hoping to climb a mountain or go on a trek in Nepal. Others might want to visit a game reserve in Africa, or do a leisurely sightseeing trip exploring the ancient ruins of Greece. A young person may want to join an under-thirties coach tour where the emphasis is on non-stop fun.

You need to establish your total budget before you start to explore the many alternatives that are available. The majority of travellers are looking for cost savings, and thanks to the internet it is possible to find some very good discounts.

The options for travel are endless and every taste and budget level is catered for, from luxury tours to low-cost camping trips. Just think of the possibilities: you could take a cruise around the Galapagos Islands, ride on the Orient Express, or do a coach tour of China or Western Europe. Perhaps you would like to do a Caribbean cruise, or take some cooking lessons in Italy.

You can travel independently, arranging your own accommodation and transport from one location to another. That gives you total flexibility and the freedom to choose whatever you want to see and experience on any given day. Be cautious about driving in other countries – it can be a hair-raising and dangerous experience and you don't want to be involved in a collision while you're on the trip of a lifetime. Avoid that and try using trains, ferries and other modes of public transport instead. They are usually both efficient and comfortable, and you can relax and enjoy the scenery while you're travelling.

Escorted tours, generally by coach, are a great way to see the best sights in the most efficient way possible. They are ideal for your first trip overseas or when you have a limited time. On my first trip to Europe many years ago, I took an escorted coach tour that visited about eight countries in fifteen days, including France, Germany, Austria, Switzerland, Italy, Luxembourg and the Netherlands.

Cruises are extremely popular, and it is no wonder when you consider the advantages. After boarding the ship, you unpack your luggage in your own stateroom. Then you sail in great comfort from one port to another with all meals and entertainment included onboard. They also sail past some stunning coastal scenery. Look at some of the itineraries that are available – you will be pleasantly surprised.

Tip 2: Avoid peak times

Try to avoid the peak travel times. That is generally when the weather is at its warmest, but when you will also encounter crowds, long lines for entry into any tourist site and the highest prices for flights and hotels. The cheapest prices will be found in the low season, but the weather can be adverse and many attractions and accommodation facilities may be closed. The shoulder season can be an ideal time to travel, with milder weather, moderate prices and smaller crowds.

Cruises tend to operate at the most pleasant time of year in any region, so your best option for lower prices will be early or late in the season. For instance, Alaskan cruises usually operate throughout the summer, but you can find cheaper prices and lighter crowds in May and September. Repositioning cruises, where ships sail from one region to another at the start of a season, are often inexpensive. Many of those involve sailing from one continent to another.

Tip 3: Use the internet to become your own travel agent

Thirty years ago, most overseas trips were booked with the help of a travel agent. As with many other activities, the internet has led to some dramatic changes in the travel industry. There are thousands of travel-related websites, in addition to the more conventional shopfront travel agencies that have existed for decades. You can now book directly with most hotels, airlines, cruise lines and tour companies, either by telephone or online – effectively becoming your own travel agent.

Travel agents provide a good service and will gladly offer advice and take care of all the bookings for you. They may also have access to some special deals of their own. If you are more comfortable with that approach, then by all means take advantage of their service. Try to ensure that you use a reputable and well-established agency, and check with friends for their recommendations. Most agencies will also operate a website where bookings can be made.

The approach I generally take is to book directly with a hotel, airline, cruise line or transport company (such as a train, ferry or bus line). They usually have their own websites that are easy to use.

Be sure to read all the fine print in your travel contracts, and make note of when final payments are due. You are often required to pay in advance, and may not get your money back if you later cancel. One way to cope with that is to take out cancellation insurance, but weigh up your options and make the appropriate decision for your own situation.

Tip 4: Shop until you drop to find the best prices

By shopping around on the internet, you can find the lowest prices and even discover some great bargains. Here is a rundown of some of the basic steps to finding the lowest prices.

Most airlines, hotel chains, cruise lines and transport companies such as coach lines or car hire companies will have a complimentary loyalty scheme. Be sure to join these before you make a booking, and you will then be able to gain access to discounted prices and perhaps accrue points or other benefits.

Flights are usually cheapest when booked well in advance. Airlines sell off a percentage of their seats at the cheapest price and, once they are sold out, fares increase as the departure date approaches. Flights will also be cheaper on certain days of the week and at different times of the year. Airlines will also offer special deals for short periods of time, so you could subscribe to receive email notifications about those. Remember that while most airlines have excellent safety standards these days, some are budget or low cost carriers while others are premium airlines with more spacious seats and meals, checked-in luggage and entertainment included. The different classes, such as economy or business class, on a budget carrier will not be equivalent to the same level on a premium airline – so take that into consideration when comparing fares.

There are several websites that compare dozens of airlines to find you the cheapest available flights on the day you want to fly. If direct flights to your destination are expensive, you may be able to fly to an alternative location at a much better price and take a cheaper flight from there.

One-way airfares can be alarmingly expensive, but they are sometimes required for a cruise. Compare the prices offered by different airlines, or you may be able to take an indirect route at a lower price.

Accommodation can be in traditional hotels, but there are many other options such as youth hostels, camping sites, rented houses or apartments, house swaps, short-term lodging booked through sites such as Airbnb, and Bed and Breakfast accommodation. Hotel booking websites are now very popular, with some offering comparisons from a number of hotel booking sites. Most of the hotels will have their own website where you can make bookings. These will often have the cheapest rates, especially if there are discounts from their loyalty schemes. The one drawback for many bookings is that you often need to pay in advance for the lowest rates. Check the terms to see if you are able to get a refund.

Cruises usually drop in price in steady increments over time as the departure date approaches, and the cost will depend on the popularity of the cruise. Cruise lines always aim to sell every berth as they make most of their profits from onboard spending. Those extras include shopping, shore excursions, drinks, gambling at the casino, spa treatments, and surcharges for some of the restaurants and activities. If you are keen to take a particular cruise, don't leave it too late to book or you may miss out.

Cruises in the past traditionally had two dinner seatings per night, and passengers would be assigned a table for the entire cruise. Although most still retain this, many now have a flexible dining option as well. The later you leave it to book a cruise, the more likely you are to find that the set dining option is booked out, and you will also have less choice of staterooms.

Check the best deals at several cruise agency websites and cruise lines. You will be able to take advantage of the best bargains if you have full flexibility with dates. That way, you can opt to book a cruise when you see a low price, often close to the departure date. If you are keen to take a particular cruise on a certain date, then you can't leave it too late or you may miss out. You also need to consider the cost of flights, as these tend to rise in price as the departure date approaches.

There is a wide range of different types of escorted tours available including coach, train, rail, walking and trekking tours. You can book through travel agencies, including online agencies, or directly with the company, but it pays to shop around. While there are often "early bird" discounts available for bookings well in advance, prices can drop substantially closer to the departure date. Once again, look for the best deals and remember that a tour may sell out if you wait too long for the lowest price.

Tip 5: Read reviews

When choosing a hotel or making any other travel booking, be sure to read reviews about it first. TripAdvisor is a well-known site that has millions of reviews written by ordinary people on just about everything to do with travel, including attractions. If you look up almost any hotel in the world, for instance, you are likely to see at least a few reviews – and perhaps hundreds. Many travellers also post photographs. Most travel websites will include reviews by customers – some favourable and some unfavourable - and they are now considered to be a vital resource.

Make use of reviews to help guide your choice and adopt the strategy of reading between the lines. For instance, you may look up a hotel and find a couple of hundred reviews. Remember that there will always be a customer who is not satisfied or may have had a bad experience due to an unavoidable incident. Don't be swayed by one bad review if all the rest are glowing, but if there are many then be wary. Check the date of the review, as recent ones are more relevant. They often include remarks about the local area and whether a hotel is in a convenient location. Look at the hotel's own photo gallery but also look at traveller photos to gain some perspective on what the hotel rooms are really like.

I recently read reviews about a hotel in Berlin, and discovered that there was a shopping centre and plenty of restaurants nearby, and it was next to a stop for the Hop-On Hop-Off sightseeing bus. That sealed the deal for me.

You can read reviews not only for hotels, but also for many attractions, airlines, cruise ships and other means of transport.

Tip 6: Research locations and transport options

Before booking accommodation, tours or cruises, you can use the internet to research the location and most convenient transport options. That will help you to streamline your journey. For instance, on an upcoming trip to Rome, I found a good deal on a hotel a few minutes walk from the airport terminal. I will be stopping there for two nights before an early morning departure to another location, and will be able to use a free hotel shuttle to the centre of Rome for sightseeing on my one full day there. On a recent trip to London, I arrived at Heathrow Airport, caught a National Express coach to Victoria Train Station and then walked a few hundred metres to my hotel.

Tip 7: Work out the best value for you

Weigh up the pros and cons before making a booking to work out whether it represents the best value for you. There are some great bargains to be found, but that may come at the cost of customer service. For instance, you may have to pay extra for checked-in luggage and meals on a budget airline. On the other hand, you may prefer to pay much more to ensure that you are looked after in comfort and style.

Tip 8: Don't underestimate your expenses

Decide on the overall budget for your trip early in the planning phase and try to calculate all your expenses. It is easy to fall into the trap of underestimating them, especially if you're a first-time traveller. As well as the cost of flights, tours or cruises and accommodation, you also need to do some research to find out the likely cost of meals, drinks, tips, optional tours, admission fees and transport.

After taking all your expenses into consideration, you may decide to opt for better value for some of the components.

Exchange rates can be confusing, and banks often charge foreign transaction fees. Write a list of the currencies that you will need and the approximate exchange rates. You can then refer to that when making a transaction, to help ensure that you are not overcharged or given the incorrect change. Familiarise yourself with the notes and coins so that you don't accidentally overspend.

My 10 Top Tips for Surviving a Long-Haul Flight

Here are my ten top tips to help you endure a long airplane flight and arrive at your destination only slightly the worse for wear.

Ah, the agony and the ecstasy. I love living in Australia, a beautiful country filled with incredible vacation spots. But I also love travelling overseas, and that generally means taking a long-haul flight. Travelling to Europe requires at least two legs totalling twenty-four hours, and it takes fourteen hours to fly from from Sydney to Los Angeles. By the end of a trip like that, every passenger on the plane looks tired and dishevelled. Over the years I have learned to cope by using a few simple strategies that will help you survive the flight and recover as quickly as possible.

Tip 1: Select your flight with care

I remember meeting a lady on a cruise around New Zealand who said that she was exhausted after spending all night on a plane. She had not realised that the flight from America would take fifteen hours, or that there was a time zone difference of almost twelve hours.

Don't let that happen to you! When you book your flights, check the times of departure and arrival as well as the expected duration. If there is more than one leg, make sure that there is sufficient time between each one. That will allow you to freshen up and reach the boarding gate even if the first flight is delayed. It's better to be waiting an hour or two in an airport terminal than to turn up after the gates are closed. On the other hand, if you can't avoid a long delay between flights, then you may be able to make use of a transit hotel for a shower and rest.

Tip 2: Upgrade if possible

There is no doubt that premium economy or business class provides far more comfort than economy class, and the spacious seats often stretch out into a fully reclined position. I'm afraid, however, that they come at a cost and you will generally find me sitting with the majority of passengers towards the rear of the plane. Rest assured, though, that if fame or fortune ever beckons then you know where I'll be sitting.

Upgrade if you feel that you need more comfort, particularly if you have a concern about your health. You will definitely have a much more enjoyable journey. Many people, however, decide that the cost is hard to justify for an ordeal that is likely to last for just a few hours.

Tip 3: Have a stopover if convenient

If you are facing a long flight then one alternative is to have a stopover. Try to divide the journey into two even legs, and make sure that where intend to stop isn't the world's most dangerous city or in the middle of a war zone. My suggestion is to stay at least two nights and have a worthwhile break. Getting off a plane, standing around waiting for your baggage and then standing in a slow line to pass through customs and immigration is quite a trial. Then you need to catch some transport to your hotel, and if you arrive in the early morning then you may need to wait several hours before you can check into your hotel room. At the end of your stopover, you face all the airport procedures again before boarding your next flight.

A few years ago it took me two torturous hours to get out of an airport terminal at two o'clock in the morning, on a stopover that lasted less than twenty-four hours. Since then I've been opting to fly straight through and get the torment over with in one fell swoop. But if you have the time then having a stopover is good decision, especially if you are travelling in economy class.

Tip 4: Wear comfortable clothes

Wear loose, comfortable clothing made of natural fibres if possible, and don't even think about wearing anything tight. Opt for layers, with a short-sleeved T-shirt and a sweatshirt. It is likely be cool on the plane, and you may also need to cope with a change of seasons.

Wear your most comfortable pair of shoes and socks, preferably trainers. Some people like to remove their shoes during the flight but I prefer to keep mine on to minimise the inevitable swelling of feet and ankles. Years ago, my poor mother took her shoes off during a long-haul flight and couldn't put them back on when it was time to disembark.

Tip 5: Schedule your medications

You need to carry medications for the flight with you, and that includes anything specifically intended for the trip, such as motion sickness treatment or sleeping tablets. If you take prescription medication, work out the change in time zones and calculate the best times to take it during the flight. When you reach your destination, you should then be able to take your medication at the same time of day as you would at home.

Tip 6: Bring a few toiletry items

Carry a few toiletry items, such as a comb, a few tissues, a travel toothbrush with toothpaste, lip balm, and a small tube of moisturiser to prevent your skin drying out. You could also take some makeup, but I suggest only a couple of essential items such as mascara and a lipstick. Due to security requirements, all of the gel and liquid items need to be placed in a small plastic ziplock bag and each container must be less than 100ml in size.

Tip 7: Avoid dehydration

It doesn't take long for dehydration to set in on a flight. Drink water, juice or soft drink throughout the journey, and if you suffer from dry eyes then take some eye drops with you. Many people refrain from drinking alcohol on a long flight, but I usually have a glass of wine with a meal. My advice, though, is to keep it to a minimum or it will interfere with your sleep and increase your rate of dehydration.

Tip 8: Exercise to stay healthy

Most airlines will have some suggested exercises listed in their safety card or in-flight magazine. Do some of those throughout the flight, particular flexing your ankles, raising and lowering your knees and moving your feet. Take any chance you can to stand up for a few minutes and try to walk around while waiting in airport terminals. All that will help to prevent deep vein thrombosis and reduce swelling of feet and ankles.

Tip 9: Get enough sleep

Try to get some sleep on the flight, and bring an eye mask if you find those beneficial. Many people also bring a neck pillow. During an overnight flight, the attendants will dim the lights at an appropriate time after the main meal has been cleared away. I'm afraid that I find it a real challenge to fall asleep in those economy class seats, while my husband somehow manages to nod off for hours.

Tip 10: Adjust to the new time zone

There is a palpable sense or relief and excitement in the cabin as a long flight comes to an end. Be sure to fill in any customs and immigration cards that you've been given, and take the chance to comb your hair and tidy up before the plane comes in to land. Make sure that you have all your belongings and, when it's time to exit, move as swiftly as you can towards the baggage claim area. Research to find out the most appropriate airport transfer service for you. Some cities have a train or coach service, or there may be a shuttle service if your hotel is near the airport.

The best way to avoid jet lag is to adjust to the time zone of your destination as quickly as possible. When you disembark, try to stay awake until close to your regular bedtime, or at least until after dinner – even if you feel like one of the walking dead. From then on, keep to a normal daily schedule and your body will soon adapt to the new time zone. If necessary, it may help to have some mild medication to help you sleep on the first night.

Now that the flight is over, the fun can really start!

My 20 Top Cruising Tips

Cruising continues to increase in popularity every year and many people keep coming back for more on a regular basis. Some are so keen that they cruise for months every year or even take up permanent residence on the high seas. It is not surprising, though, because in my view it is hard to think of a more enjoyable way to travel. Here are my twenty top tips to help you book and make the most of a cruise.

Tip 1: Weigh up the benefits of cruising

Most cruise ships have stunning décor, with a glamorous lobby, lavish restaurants and several swimming pools. There is usually a spa and fitness centre, a casino, duty-free shops and a number of lounges and bars. The staterooms are designed with comfort in mind, with well-designed closets and drawers so that you can unpack your luggage, push your suitcase under the bed and then dedicate yourself to fun and relaxation for the rest of your voyage. Entertainment is available all day, with shows, live music, guest speakers, movies and various other activities. The cuisine is regarded as a major highlight of most cruises, served à la carte or buffet style and even including snacks.

For most people, though, one of the main reasons for taking a cruise is to visit the ports. These are sometimes overnight stays, but generally a cruise ships sails into port early in the morning and departs later that day. Often, the sail in (or out) can be a stunning spectacle in its own right, but the day in port gives you a chance to see quite a few sights on your own or on a tour, and perhaps have a chance to sample the local cuisine. Then it's back on board before sailing on to the next destination – which might be in another country.

But your travel experiences aren't just limited to the port visits, because there is also likely to some scenic cruising as well. You might sail down a fjord in Norway, past a glacier in Alaska, through the Panama Canal in Central America or parallel to the Great Barrier Reef in Australia.

Tip 2: Consider the cruise length

Cruises can very widely in length. There are some for as little as one or two days, known as sampler cruises, that give you a chance to experience what cruising has to offer. Many are for a few days or up to two weeks, while you can also find some that last weeks or months. The longer ones are often called world cruises, and while there are many people who are regular devotees, others view them as a once-in-a-lifetime journey. I was lucky enough to experience a voyage across the Pacific from Sydney to Vancouver that took twenty-eight days, as well as a thirty-nine night cruise from Singapore, through the Suez Canal and on to London. Another option is to combine two or more back-to-back cruises. Two years ago, I sailed on a wonderful three-week cruise around the Mediterranean that was actually a combination of two shorter cruises.

You might think that several weeks or months is an excessive amount of time to be on a cruise ship, but it can be a very easy way to see some great sights around the world. Not surprisingly, the majority of passengers on a long voyage are in an older age bracket. Most of the passengers tend to settle into a daily routine punctuated with activities and mealtimes. Long cruises often include quite a few sea days as the ship sails from one region to another, but there will be plenty of activities to keep you busy. Remember to include some exercise, such as workout or class in the fitness centre, or walking around the deck. You could also do some swimming or take a dance class.

The cruise length will generally depend on the destination. Cruises to Alaska, the Norwegian fiords, or Canada and New England usually take about seven days, and there are many short Mediterranean cruises as the ports are reasonably close to one another.

Tip 3: Check the itinerary before booking

Before booking a cruise, always check the itinerary carefully to note the ports to be visited, including the expected time of arrival and departure. While you will visit most ports for a full day, you may occasionally pay a slightly longer visit, especially if it is major city. For instance, when I sailed on a Baltic cruise the ship was berthed overnight in St Petersburg, so that we had two days there. Occasionally, you may only visit a port for a few hours.

Also check on the number of sea days. On a shorter cruise there may be several ports plus two or three sea days. But one or more of those sea days may involve what is known as scenic cruising. On a New Zealand cruise, for example, you may sail for two days from Sydney across the Tasman Sea (that locals jokingly refer to as *the ditch*). The third day will be another sea day, but you will be doing scenic cruising for several hours in the beautiful Fiordland National Park area. Then you will proceed to visit several ports over the next few days.

Some longer cruises or ocean crossings may involve several sea days in succession, as many as seven in some cases. You don't want to sign up for a cruise and then be surprised or disappointed to find that you are spending days at sea that you had not expected. However, most people enjoy a few sea days during any cruise as there will be plenty of activities to keep you entertained or you can relax and read a book, see a movie or chat to friends.

Tip 4: Choose the style of cruising that suits you

There are dozens of cruise lines and they fall into several main categories. Luxury lines are far more expensive than most but deliver a high standard of comfort, service and cuisine. Four and five star cruise lines have an excellent standard, and there are also lines that provide a more economical but still very comfortable experience.

Each cruise line tends to have its own style of travel. Some are orientated more towards families and party-orientated activities that suit a younger crowd. Many others tend to have a more sedate atmosphere and are favoured by more mature travellers, and some lines manage to combine all of these. There are a few cruise lines aimed at adventurous travellers who want to explore unusual destinations in-depth. Some have a casual atmosphere for both days and evenings, while most will have a smart casual dress code in the evenings plus one or two formal nights per week.

When considering a cruise, use the internet to find out more about the travel style of that line to decide if that is a good fit with you. Most travel agency and cruise review websites will have information about that.

Tip 5: Decide on a cruise destination

When selecting a cruise destination, you may opt to take advantage of a great deal on a cruise that sounds interesting. On the other hand, you may be aiming to find the ideal destination for your dream vacation. Find out some information about the ports you will be visiting to help with your decision, and also consider the weather that you are likely to encounter.

These have been some my favourite cruise destinations so far:

• Alaska – for spectacular scenery and wildlife, including bears and whales

• The Norwegian Fiords – some of the most incredible terrain on Earth

• The Panama Canal – an engineering marvel

• The Mediterranean – fascinating towns and ancient ruins

• The Baltic – island-studded harbours and beautiful cities, including Copenhagen, Stockholm and St Petersburg

• New Zealand – a scenic coastline and delightful ports

Tip 6: Examine the deck plans when selecting a stateroom

The price of a cruise generally decreases as the departure date approaches, until all staterooms are booked out. When booking, you will always be asked to choose a category of stateroom, with the cheapest being an inside cabin. More expensive than that will be an oceanview cabin (which has a window), or a balcony cabin. There may be a minisuite category, which is slightly more spacious than a standard balcony cabin, and a smaller number of suites, which are far more expensive and usually have some extra benefits such as access to an exclusive restaurant and lounge.

Within each category there will be several sub-categories with better rooms costing more. You may be able to see the staterooms that are still available so you can choose the one that best appeals to you.

Alternatively, you may be given a "guaranteed cabin." This guarantees you a stateroom at a specific sub-category, and the room number will be allocated closer to the sailing date.

Before opting for a specific room or sub-category, check the deck plans and examine all the features. This will tell you if the room is an odd shape, has a porthole instead of a picture window or any other features that would not suit you. See where the room is located: is it close to the elevator, or near an area that you fear may be noisy? Rooms in the midship tend to be more stable than those in the forward or aft sections.

You should also be able to find some YouTube videos and reviews from ordinary people to give you insights on the staterooms and the rest of the ship. For instance, if you are considering a balcony cabin, chances are that a couple of previous passengers have posted a home movie tour of the same type of cabin.

Tip 7: Select set or flexible dining

Most cruise ships used to have two dinner seatings in the main dining room each night, at around 6 pm and 8 pm, and passengers would be assigned a table at one of these for the duration of their cruise. That still occurs on most cruise ships, but many have cut back and only assign about half the passengers to those. The rest are allocated to flexible dining, which means you can reserve a table at any time of the evening – and many people prefer that option. Some cruise lines only offer flexible dining, and most have several specialty restaurants that have a surcharge. However, you are not obliged to eat there and can usually opt to dine in the main dining room. Some passengers prefer to eat in the buffet restaurant, and there are also other options such as in-room dining.

If you have flexible dining or want to try a specialty restaurant, you may be able to reserve a table online up to several weeks in advance. I recently reserved a table in the main dining room at 7.30 pm for every night of an upcoming cruise.

Tip 8: Take advantage of special deals

The hard truth about cruising is that you also need to pay for drinks, gratuities and all other onboard spending. But a number of cruise lines have recently had some great deals that include free pre-paid gratuities, a beverage package, an onboard spending credit and perhaps even free WiFi or dining at a specialty restaurant. It is worth shopping around to see if any special offers are available.

Tip 9: What to pack for your cruise

Always check the expected temperatures to see whether you'll need warm or light clothing. During the day, casual clothes are the norm – and don't forget to pack a swimming costume, and also a hat and comfortable walking shoes for port days. In temperate zones it can be chilly, or downright freezing, on the decks, especially once you get out to sea. Be sure to bring a jumper and warm jacket.

The dress code for most evenings is usually smart casual. Many cruise lines have one or two formal nights per week, but a simple cocktail dress is acceptable for women and many men wear a suit rather than a dinner suit (tuxedo). The cruise line website will have information about the dress code on your ship, and it is expected that everyone adhere to the nightly code even if you are dining in the buffet restaurant.

Tip 10: Explore the ship after boarding

When you board the ship, put your cabin bag in your stateroom and then enjoy some lunch in the buffet restaurant. Your luggage is likely to be delivered to your stateroom later in the afternoon, so take the time to explore the ship. Check the IT area if you would like to connect to the internet – there may be an opening special available.

There will always be a compulsory muster drill before departure. Find out the time and location and be sure not to miss it.

When your luggage is delivered, unpack and make yourself at home. There should be plenty of drawers and closet space for everything, including shelves in the bathroom for all your toiletries. Lock your passport, wallet, jewellery and other valuables in the room safe. Then you can stow your suitcase under the bed.

Your keycard can be used for any purchases onboard. You will be encouraged to purchase photographs, have spa treatments, shop or go to the casino – but remember that none of these are compulsory. I usually find that my favourite perfume is available in one of the stores at a very competitive price.

There may be a laundry room available, but they are slowly disappearing from most cruise ships. Embarkation day is a good time to make use of them, as you will probably be the only person there. You can usually have a bag of laundry washed for about twenty or twenty-five dollars, or you can wash a few small items each day in the bathroom sink.

Tip 11: Staying connected is getting easier

These days, many of us find it hard to live without access to the internet, so many people sign up to use the internet service at sea. It is very expensive, but the price has come down in recent years and the speed and quality has improved. You should be able log in and use the internet in your own stateroom, but connectivity may be better in public areas and you will probably find that streaming services may be blocked. The speed will be better at times of low usage such as late at night, early morning, or during mealtimes. Always remember to log off when you are finished.

If you want to avoid those high charges, you can utilise WiFi facilities when you visit ports – or try having a complete break from the internet for a few days.

Tip 12: Take simple measures to stay healthy

Have all the vaccines recommended by your doctor before travelling. While on board, wash your hands frequently and take advantage of hand sanitisers around the ship. Remember that handles and railings carry a heavy load of germs, so only use them when necessary and avoid putting your hands near your mouth. If you have a cold or gastrointestinal bug, try to keep yourself isolated and avoid anyone who appears unwell.

Tip 13: Be sure to check the daily guide

Check your daily guide each night and use a highlighter to mark the activities that interest you for the following day. The dress code for dinner will also be listed.

On the night before a port visit there should also be tourist information. Be sure to check the expected arrival and boarding times, and also what documents you need to take ashore. Often, you will only need to carry a photo identification card, such as your driver's licence, but sometimes you may need to carry your passport. You will always need to take your keycard, and be sure to scan it as you leave and return to the ship.

Tip 14: Take advantage of the dining options

Read about the dining options before your cruise. There will always be an à la carte main dining room which should be open for breakfast, lunch and dinner. The buffet restaurant is popular choice for breakfast and lunch, and some people opt to have dinner there as well. There may be other complimentary dining choices including cafes, a pizza bar and several specialty restaurants that have a surcharge. Room service meals should also be available.

If you would like to dine at a specialty restaurant, you should be able to book online in advance if you are keen to secure a specific date or time.

Tip 15: Examine alternatives for exploring ports

When in port, you can opt to do a shore excursion organised by the ship, but do some internet research about the port to find out what the key highlights are and what aspects may interest you. For instance, when I visited the port of Kirkwall, on the Orkney Islands, I knew that I wanted to see Skara Brae, the remains of a Neolithic village. I therefore opted for a ship's tour that included a visit to that historic site which was seventeen miles from the town.

The ideal situation for a port visit is when you are berthed right in the heart of a town. If the city centre is a short distance away, a shuttle may be provided for passengers, often with a small fee, or there may be a convenient means of public transport. A year ago, I stopped at the port of Cobh in Ireland. There was a small train station right next to the quayside with a pleasant twenty-five minute train ride to the small city of Cork.

If you opt for a private tour, check reviews or get recommendations from friends. The most important thing to remember is to be back on the ship before the all-aboard time. If you are on one of the organised shore excursions, the ship will wait for you if there is a delay. But if you are on your own or taking a privately-arranged tour and are late returning, then you will need to wave good-bye as the ship sails off into the sunset, and find your own way to the next port.

The final aspect to consider is that weather or adverse sailing conditions can prevent the ship from docking in a port, or delay the arrival. If that happens and you have arranged a private tour, then you will need to be able to contact the company to cancel or make alternative arrangements.

My rule of thumb is to tour independently if possible, walking around to discover all the highlights by myself. But if the major attractions that I am keen to see are some distance away then I will take a ship's tour. I was once lucky enough to visit Aqaba in Jordan on a long cruise from Singapore to Europe. Because the incredible ruins of Petra were nearly two hours drive away, I chose to take a shore excursion.

I'll be talking more about exploring any destination in the next chapter.

Tip 16: Discover the bars and lounges that suit your style

There should be several bars on your cruise ship, each with their own atmosphere and décor. That will include open air and poolside bars, cosy and comfortable lounges, and enclosed upper deck areas with an expansive view. Some will have musical entertainment and a dance floor, or function as a night club. Find the ones that appeal to you, or try them all – and remember that you are not obliged to order a drink, and can also opt to order a soda.

Tip 17: Catch tenders early

At some ports, cruise ships will dock offshore and use tenders to transport people to the shore. They generally use the lifeboats or hire small ferries that you will board from one of the lower decks. There is no need to be concerned about this process. There will always be at least two crew members to provide assistance as passengers step on and off, and those with any physical disabilities are well looked after. While there may be sometimes issues with delays, the ship's crew will be aiming to transport you to and from the port as quickly as possible.

To avoid delays and long lines, try to catch a tender as early as possible in the morning, and then return to the ship well before boarding time.

Tip 18: Pre-pay gratuities

You will need to pay gratuities, and there is normally a standard amount charged to your account. That is likely to be about thirteen dollars a day per passenger, which covers not only your stewards and dining attendants but also other behind-the-scenes staff such as general cleaning staff, kitchen hands and laundry staff. You can opt to pre-pay these gratuities, or it may be included in your fare in some cases. If you prefer to give your tips to service staff in person, or discuss other issues about tipping, then speak to the front desk about it.

Tip 19: Avoid arguments

If you have any complaints about another passenger, then avoid speaking to or confronting them about it. Report the situation to the front desk, either in person or by telephone, for the matter to be resolved. Anyone who engages in an argument or other disruptive activities may face being removed from the ship at the next port.

Tip 20: Be sure to plan your disembarkation

A few days before your cruise ends, you should receive information about the disembarkation process. Be sure to complete the form and hand it in well ahead of time. There will a number of options to choose from, including the time you wish to leave the ship, and there will also be offers to transfer you to the airport or city centre. If you are not flying out until later that day, there may be an airport transfer available that includes a sightseeing tour en route.

You will need to leave your luggage out the night before your cruise ends, unless you opt to walk it off the ship yourself.

My 10 Tips for Exploring Any Destination

Whether you are visiting for the day on a cruise, or you have arrived by plane, train, automobile or any other means – here are my ten top tips for exploring any new destination.

Tip 1: Find out about safety and security

Do some research before you travel to find out about the safety and security situation. Your own government's Department or Ministry of Foreign Affairs (or U.S. Department of State) should have an A-Z listing of all countries with travel warnings and recommendations, including health information. If they advise against visiting a destination, then you should consider changing your plans.

Tip 2: Choose convenient accommodation

Before booking any accommodation, find it on a map and see how close it is to the main attractions. If it is located some distance away, find out if there are convenient transport options nearby, and also shops and eateries. That will enable you to make the best use of your time.

Tip 3: Dress for comfort

You may only have a few hours at a location and the weather may work against you, so don't forget to bring some rain gear. Make sure you have a folding umbrella and a poncho or water-resistant raincoat with a hood. Also have a plastic carry bag to deposit the wet items whenever you retreat inside.

Comfortable walking shoes are a must, and bring a spare pair if possible in case the first pair gets wet or muddy.

Tip 4: Bring some local currency

If possible, bring some foreign currency with you to give you a head start when you arrive at a new destination. In places that are known to readily accept American dollars, such as Central America, be sure you have plenty of small denominations as the vendors and taxi drivers are unlikely to be able to give you change.

Tip 5: Do some research to discover the highlights

There are many tourism websites that will provide information about the main highlights of any destination. But sometimes the information is split into different sub-categories such as: *families, museums, adventure, historical.* You are then forced to open multiple pages and still not be able to clarify what you should be aiming to see in a short space of time. Move on to other sites or articles that will give you a concise list of the top ten or twenty sights that should not be missed.

Tip 6: Read blog articles by other tourists

Supplement your research by reading a couple of blog articles written by real tourists. Search for a few alternatives such as: *a day in Avignon* or *my visit to Edinburgh.* These will often give you a rundown of the best sights with some photographs, plus practical suggestions, such as how to use the local transportation.

Tip 7: Take a Hop-On Hop-Off bus

Many popular towns and cities have a Hop-On Hop-Off bus service that will take tourists on a circuit with stops at the local points of interest. There will be a detailed commentary and you can get off as many times as you like, explore and return later to catch the next bus. In some cases there may be several companies offering a similar service and, in the biggest cities, there may be more than one loop. In New York, for instance, there is a circuit of lower Manhattan and another one for upper Manhattan.

Although more expensive than public transport, they are an excellent way to see as much as you can in the shortest time possible, hassle-free and with the least wear and tear on your feet.

Tip 8: Explore on your own

My favourite way to experience any new destination is to wander around the heart of town, discovering what lies in store around every corner. Many towns in Europe have narrow streets lined with historic buildings, so walking is the only viable way to explore them. Always be security conscious and don't head down dark, deserted lanes. But unless you are advised that it is unsafe to do so, never hesitate to get out there and see the sights on your own.

Try to obtain a free map at your arrival point such as a train station or airport, or from the welcoming party when you disembark a cruise. Alternatively, you should be able to find one at your hotel or the local visitor information centre.

Tip 9: Take a sightseeing tour

An organised sightseeing tour will give you a chance to see the highlights or explore attractions that might be located away from the city centre. Visitor information centres, your hotel or travel agent will be able to advise you. If you book a tour yourself, be sure to read reviews or get recommendations from friends.

Tip 10: Use combo-tickets to visit the main attractions

In major tourist destinations, various combination passes are often available that give you admission to a number of attractions. They can provide great cost-savings compared to the price of individual tickets, but make sure that you will be able to take full advantage of them before making your purchase.

My 5 Top Tips for Escorted Tours

In an escorted tour you will be looked after by a guide and generally travel by coach to a number of destinations, with sightseeing and many meals included, as well as luggage handling and perhaps transfers from the airport. It is a great way to see as many sights as possible in the least amount of time, with all the travel arrangements taken care of for you.

Here are my five top tips for making the most of an escorted tour.

Tip 1: Check the itinerary before you book

Examine the itinerary carefully before you make any bookings, and choose a tour that is best suited to your tastes and physical capacities.

Some are aimed at younger or more active travellers, while others may be slow-paced and leisurely. Budget tours may have more economical accommodation that is located at a distance from the main sights, while luxury tours will use four or five star hotels and have a range of extra inclusions. Many escorted tours will be quite busy, visiting two or three locations in a day and with some walking involved. There is sure to be some time spent on the main highways if you are travelling long distances, but there will also be times when you follow the scenic routes.

Tip 2: Avoid motion sickness

If you are prone to motion sickness, then bring some mild medication as you are likely to encounter windy roads at some stage of the journey. Discuss the best treatment options with your doctor or pharmacist and ask your guide each day about the likely traffic conditions. Try to take the medication beforehand to prevent you from becoming nauseous.

Always carry a small water bottle and some boiled candies. You may also want to bring some wet wipes and a small ziplock plastic bag in case of emergencies.

Tip 3: Be punctual

Remember to pack an alarm clock or use the one on your smartphone, as you will probably need to be up early on many occasions. Make sure that you have a watch and always try to be punctual so that the tour runs smoothly for everyone. If you intend to head off on your own at any stage and not return to the coach, then let your guide know so that the other passengers are not left waiting for you.

Have a small notebook and pen in your handbag or coat pocket to jot down meeting times, as it is easy to forget these. When given free time to explore a destination on your own, don't lose track of time and try to avoid getting lost. Ask directions if you are uncertain, and take a photo of your bus and hotel – you can show those if there is a language barrier.

Tip 4: Don't try to do too much

While you may be keen to see everything that you possibly can, don't be tempted to overdo it. There will usually be various optional tours offered but you are not obliged to sign up for all of them. They will add significantly to the cost of your trip so choose the ones that appeal to you or that sound like a worthwhile experience. You may become overtired after several days of early starts and long days on the road, so it may be preferable to relax or get an early night.

Tip 5: Don't have unrealistic expectations

Most escorted tours are designed to help you see as much as possible in the allowed time, but you will never be able to see everything that each destination has to offer. Don't build your expectations up to fever pitch, as you are still in real life and there may occasionally be hiccups. With good luck, everything will run smoothly and the guide should be able to help you with any issues or difficulties that might arise.

My Travel Preparation Checklist

30 things to do before an overseas trip

You have booked your trip and can hardly wait to set off. But there are still quite a few very important chores to complete before you leave home. Here is my comprehensive list of things to do before almost any overseas trip. Some of these may not apply to you, or you may have additional items of your own, but it will give you a basis for compiling your own checklist. If you have booked a fully escorted tour, many of the travel arrangements mentioned will be included in that.

Let's say that you have decided to take a cruise or a coach tour, and have paid a deposit to secure the booking. Now, let's proceed from there. This checklist takes you right up to the moment when you shut your front door and head off on that incredible journey.

Checklist

1. Prepare your own itinerary document with each day of your trip listed, and add your your travel arrangements.

2. Book flights and selects seats.

3. Book any additional escorted tours or cruises.

4. Research transfers to airports or ports and book those if necessary.

5. Book other transport, such as trains, coaches or ferries, and any car hire.

6. Book accommodation.

7. Buy travel insurance in case you require emergency medical treatment while overseas.

8. Do research on each destination that you will be visiting, including cruise ports, to find out about the main tourist highlights.

9. Book any shore excursions or other sightseeing tours that you have selected.

10. Purchase admission tickets in advance to attractions that you

intend to visit if there are clear advantages to doing so, such as a cost saving or being able to avoid standing in a long line to gain entry. Remember, if you are doing a sightseeing tour then admission prices are usually included.

11. Complete the online check-in process for cruises and escorted tours.

12. Obtain any visas if necessary. Check with the relevant embassies in your country and email or telephone them if you have any questions. Some countries may not require a visa but there may be an online form to complete, such as the ESTA for the United States.

13. Make the final payment for any cruises or escorted tours on or before the due date.

14. Print boarding documents and luggage tags for cruises and other tours. The tags will need to be stapled around the handles of your luggage so remember to pack a small stapler.

15. If you don't have a set dining table on a cruise, you may be able to make an online reservation for a table each night, even in the complimentary main dining room. However, you will also be able to do that onboard if you prefer. There will be other items that you can book in advance as well, such as beverage packages or spa treatments. You can also pre-pay gratuities.

16. Obtain small amounts of foreign currency if you would like to have some on hand when you arrive at a destination. Purchase a money travel card and load it with foreign currency or make other arrangements for your expenses while overseas. Try to see if you can obtain a credit card that does not charge foreign transaction fees.

17. Notify your banks that you will be overseas, so that they are aware that you may be making foreign transactions.

18. Make arrangements for using your mobile phone while overseas. To avoid hefty fees, turn off data roaming before you travel if you don't intend to use it.

19. Organise boarding for your pets.

20. Arrange for the collection or holding of your mail.

21. Obtain a letter from your doctor listing all your medication.

Make sure that you have enough medications to last for your entire trip (plus a few spare days) and carry them in your hand luggage in their original packaging.

22. Investigate the travel adapter plugs that you will require, or purchase a universal one.

23. Edit your trip itinerary to include all your travel details and prepare a slim folder that includes all your travel documents, such as tickets, hotel vouchers, cruise and tour documents and information on each destination. Also include the letter from your doctor, travel insurance documents, and a photocopy of your passport. Send a copy of all these documents to cloud storage in case your folder or computer device is lost or stolen.

24. Email a copy of your travel itinerary including your contact details in case of emergency to a close family member or friend, and notify anyone else who needs to know about your absence.

25. Arrange for the payment of bills while away.

26. Research the expected average monthly temperatures for all your destinations and prepare a luggage list. (See the next chapter for more information on your travel packing).

27. Arrange for watering of pot plants and garden maintenance while away.

28. Run down perishable food items in your fridge and pantry.

29. Pack your luggage and make sure you have everything on your list, including cords for your electronic devices. Don't forget your passport, visas, wallet, medications, spectacles and itinerary folder.

30. Do a final check of your house to make sure that all switches are turned off, trash emptied, and doors and windows locked. Turn off all alarms and other gadgets that you have pre-set to switch on automatically.

Shut the front door, and you are on your way!

My Travel Packing Tips

How to pack for an overseas trip

There are two extremes of the travel packing spectrum, and I don't fall into either one of those. At one end is the backpacker or those who can pack enough for several weeks travel in a small bag and toss it into an overhead locker inside a plane cabin. At the other end of the spectrum are those with a giant suitcase or two packed with enough clothes to do a royal tour.

For years I erred on the side of excess, taking more clothes than I needed. Somehow, everything inside my suitcase somehow managed to double in volume, so that by the end of the journey I could barely close it. Despite making feeble efforts to keep everything tidy, the contents became increasingly dishevelled as time went on.

One day the crisis came. Boarding a flight from Seattle to Los Angeles, I was charged two hundred dollars in excess baggage fees for being one or two kilos over the weight limit. Filled with dismay, I vowed that would never happen again.

Some people can survive an overseas trip armed only with two pairs of jeans, three Tshirts, two sweatshirts and a jacket. But if you are taking a cruise, a few smarter outfits for evening wear are usually required, and many cruises also have one or two formal nights per week. That means you will need to take a suitcase, but with some careful planning you can keep it to a minimum and still be well dressed.

Here are my suggestions for your travel packing list. The key to success is to choose items that are light in weight, stretchy and uncrushable. Layer clothes to cope with a combination of cool and warm weather, and choose tops that can also be worn in the evening.

Try to stick with a small range of colours that all co-ordinate. Choose tops that match all your pants or skirts and dress them up with a scarf or jacket. The same items can then be mixed and matched to create several different outfits.

Choosing Luggage

There are three items of luggage that I generally take on an overseas trip lasting two or more weeks: a suitcase, a small cabin bag and a handbag.

I believe in having a suitcase of good quality and moderate size, and I don't opt for the highly expensive and super-sized varieties. My goal is to keep my luggage to a minimum, and if I filled a huge suitcase full to the brim, then it would be a heavy load to lug around and would incur exhorbitant excess-baggage fees. During any overseas trip, it undergoes a huge ordeal as it is dragged around from one location to another, thrown around by luggage handlers and squashed under other bags. The wear and tear eventually takes it toll and your suitcase will need to be replaced, so there is no need to invest too much money in one.

I recommend a cross body style handbag with wide, sturdy straps and zippered openings. Wear it in front of you so that you can see it, and keep a firm hold of it, all the time. My cabin bag is a small carry bag with a shoulder strap that can be secured to the handle of my suitcase when walking.

My Travel Handbag

The last thing I want to do while exploring a new destination is to be weighted down by my handbag, like the ancient mariner with an albatross around his neck. However, there are a few key items that I always need to have on hand. These include my passport, wallet, a lipstick, lip balm, a comb, a little pocket pack of tissues, camera, sunglasses, spectacles, my phone and the travel information or vouchers required for that day. Last but not least, a pen comes in handy for making notes and completing forms.

I organise my wallet before leaving home, and remove any cards that I won't be using overseas. You will need a driver's licence as a form of photo ID, even if you won't be driving, and also any foreign currency that you obtained in advance.

There are small bags for men, but if that is not your style then there are money belts and travel pouches available that are designed for keeping a passport and wallet safe.

My Cabin Bag

My cabin bag is carried when travelling from one destination to another, but it stays in my hotel room or stateroom when not in transit. Packed inside are important items that I don't want to leave in my suitcase. That includes medications for the entire trip, a zippered pouch with jewellery, and electronic devices and cords - my mobile phone, a kindle for reading ebooks, my laptop computer, a small camera with the charging cord and a spare battery, and travel adapter plugs. I also like to bring my sonic toothbrush, which comes with a small travel case and charging cord.

Finally, I bring a folding zippered jacket in case of cold weather, a spare T-shirt and a folding umbrella. I also include the toiletry items I need for a long-haul flight, and place gels and liquids in a ziplock plastic bag to satisfy security requirements.

Packing Your Suitcase

Years ago, by the time I was a few days into any trip, the interior of my suitcase would be in a state of complete chaos. Now I use zippered travel packing bags to keep everything in order.

All my toiletry items fit into one soft-sided toiletry bag, including makeup, cleansing cream and moisturiser, body lotion, comb and styling wand, toothbrush, toothpaste and dental floss, cotton buds, little shower cap and a disposal razor. We all have our own list of essential toiletry items, and remember that if you're staying in a hotel then soap, shampoo and a hairdryer will usually be supplied.

Rather than folding your clothes flat, try the new technique of rolling them. It is amazing how much more you can fit into the same space, and you can then place them in small packing bags.

Check the average temperatures that you are likely to encounter on your trip. Put lighter items at the bottom, and place heavier items on top to keep them in place.

Here are two packing lists that I used – one for winter, and one for summer. Gentlemen, I hope, will be able to compile their packing list by following the same principles, with layers of comfortable, light clothing.

Packing list for a summer trip to Europe, including a cruise

- 2 pairs of jeans and 2 other pairs of lightweight trousers
- 5 short-sleeved tops and 2 long-sleeved tops
- 2 soft scarves
- comfortable and sturdy walking shoes
- ballets flats for evening
- swimming gear
- 3 shift dresses for evening
- 2 tops and 1 pair of dress pants for evening
- 1 cocktail dress and comfortable heels for formal nights on cruise
- pashmina and cardigan
- nighties and underwear
- sunhat
- small selection of costume jewellery
- small stapler and staples for attaching luggage tags for cruise

Packing list for a winter trip to Europe, including a cruise

I was lucky enough to take a winter cruise around the Mediterranean a couple of years ago, and had a wonderful time. The weather was cool but mild, which made it ideal for walking, and there were no crowds. Here is what I packed.

- a light but warm padded coat
- 3 pairs of warm trousers including jeans
- 5 long-sleeved tops and 4 woollen sweaters (which can also be used in the evening)
- 3 winter scarves

- comfortable and sturdy walking shoes
- black ankle boots – for both day and evening
- 2 pencil skirts with black tights, and 1 pair of smart trousers, for evening
- 1 warm cocktail dress for evening
- 1 smart winter top for evening (and also use tops and sweaters worn during the day)
- 1 cocktail dress and comfortable heels for formal night on cruise
- pashmina
- winter nighties and underwear
- snug winter hat and gloves
- small selection of costume jewellery
- small stapler and staples for attaching luggage tags for cruise

A final note

My goal is to have a good selection of outfits and everything I need for a comfortable trip, but still have the weight of my suitcase well below eighteen kilograms. Another aim is to keep the contents neat and well organised by using packing bags. The ultimate purpose for all that is to keep my focus on enjoying every moment of my journey, rather than being burdened with a mountain of luggage.

My 6 Top Tips for Travel Safety

Wherever you are in the world, including your own home, it always pays to be security conscious and to consider your own health and safety. Here are my six top tips for travel safety – and they are matters of the utmost importance.

Tip 1: Travel Insurance

Never travel overseas without having travel insurance: it is absolutely essential. If you cannot afford it, then please do not travel. The insurance covers you for accidents and emergency medical and dental care, including the cost of evacuating you back home if that ever became necessary.

Medical bills overseas, and the cost of medical evacuations, can be horrifyingly high. Those without insurance often face bills of hundreds of thousands of dollars and hospitals will insist on payment. Some people are trapped in a foreign country because they cannot afford to pay the cost of being evacuated home. Can you imagine the financial or personal devastation that could cause you or your family if you were in that situation?

Tip 2: Personal Security

Be security conscious at all times when travelling overseas. Some areas, such as the Mediterranean cities that are crowded with tourists, are renowned for pickpockets. Men should keep their passport and wallet inside their coat pocket or secured to their body with a money belt. Women should carry a cross body style handbag with a wide, sturdy strap, and have it zipped up and in front of them at all times.

Don't wear flashy jewellery and keep your camera or phone secured to your body. Do not be distracted by taking photographs or seeing the sights, and never put your bag down anywhere, or open it in public. Be aware of the people around you, and don't walk through deserted laneways or empty parks. Stick to where there are plenty of people around, but don't let anyone get to close to you. Be extremely cautious at night, and preferably only travel by vehicle.

Read your own government's travel advisory information for any country that you intend to visit. Be sure to avoid any protests or demonstrations, and don't become involved in any political issues. Avoid getting into any arguments, and never be tempted to take any drugs. Laws in other countries can be very harsh.

I am afraid that you tend to be more of a target if you are elderly and slow. Keep a sharp lookout and don't allow a group of people, including children, to surround you.

Tip 3: Avoid Travel Scams

There are many travel scams that happen all around the world, but being forewarned can help you to avoid them. Here are just a few examples.

• Taxi scams are common. One that we have probably all experienced is to be taken on an extended journey – also known as the *scenic route* - to your destination. Check online for the standard fare for a trip, and agree on the price with the driver before getting in their vehicle. Make sure that the meter is working and appears to be operating properly – not ticking over too fast. Be aware of the exchange rate for the local currency so that you are not overcharged or given inadequate change. If you are booked into a hotel, don't believe a driver who insists that the hotel is shut and that they will take you somewhere else. If you suspect trouble, ask them to stop and get out of their vehicle.

• Tour guides and taxi drivers may sometimes try to insist on taking you to a store that supposedly has the best quality items at the best price. Respond by telling them that you are not interested in shopping.

• Be suspicious of anyone approaching you and offering to help you in some way.

• There are a variety of well-known scams, particularly in certain locations. Someone may alert you to a spillage on your clothes, then pretend to wipe the stain and deftly steal your wallet or phone. Someone may push in front of you in the airport security line and cause a delay while another person grabs your belongings from the moving belt. Another trick is when a man impersonating a policeman wants to check your passport, says there is something wrong with your visa and demands an on-the-spot payment to fix it.

• A woman may ask if you would like a drink and then, after spending an hour or two at a nearby bar, you are presented with an enormous bill – or your drink is spiked and you are robbed.

• There are many ways that a pickpocket may approach you. A woman may throw a baby at you and when you go to grab the poor child, thieves will rifle your pockets. Try not to react, as the baby will only be a doll. In the same vein as that, sometimes children will surround you, or a person falls over in front of you. Grab tight hold of your belongings and move away quickly, yelling out for help if necessary.

• Beware of people running towards you or approaching you on a motorbike. Look around frequently so that you are aware of your surroundings.

Remember that by repeating the word, "No," firmly, you will show that you are confident and aware of their tricks. The thieves will then move on to an easier target.

Tip 4: Drink Safety

It is safe to drink tap water in Europe, Australia and New Zealand, North America and many other developed countries, but always check the recommendations for your destination.

In areas without a reliable water source, it can be made safe by boiling or using purifiers. You can also drink bottled water from a well-known brand, but make sure the top is properly sealed. Don't forget that you also need to use safe water for cleaning your teeth and washing your face.

Soft drinks (sodas) should be all right to consume, but don't add ice to any drinks unless you are sure it is made from safe water.

Tip 5: Food Safety

Food is an important factor to consider in developing countries, but by following a few principles of food hygiene you can help to avoid the dangers.

The main risks are from the bacteria load on the surface of food, and in allowing warm dishes to sit around for long periods of time so that germs are allowed to multiply. That means the ideal foods are ones that are cooked quickly at high temperature, then served to you straight away. Salads and fresh fruits without a thick skin will usually be washed under running water, so they are often contaminated.

The main foods to avoid in countries with unsafe drinking water are raw or undercooked food, salads, fruit that can't be peeled, raw seafood and eggs, and unpasteurised dairy products.

It should be safe to eat food in cans or sealed packs, fresh food cooked at high temperatures, and fruit that can be peeled such as bananas.

Tip 6: Health and Injury Hazards

See your doctor several weeks before your trip to discuss your general health requirements and the need for vaccinations. You may need routine shots, plus shots for Tetanus, Hepatitis A and/or Influenza.

Some simple hygiene techniques will help to prevent the spread of infections, including colds and intestinal bugs. Wash your hands frequently with soap and running water, and avoid putting your hands near your mouth or touching your face. Railings and door handles have been shown to carry a heavy load of germs, so avoid touching them if possible. However, don't compromise your physical safety as you may need to hang on to railings to prevent falls. If you do, just wash your hands afterwards.

There are all sorts of hazards overseas that you may not be accustomed to at home. In Europe, you may encounter many cobblestone streets. In Asia, footpaths can absent or narrow and precarious. Drivers can also be extremely reckless in many countries. In the Netherlands, you need to be very wary of the many bicycles, while in parts of Asia, such as Vietnam, there are many motorbikes.

The last thing you want to do is stumble and fall, or be hit by a vehicle, while you are on vacation. Be careful while walking around, and always wear sturdy and comfortable shoes. Cobblestones can be agony in high heels or sandals.

At night, always turn on a light before walking around. In an unfamiliar room, it is easy to become disorientated in darkness, and the consequences of a fall can be devastating. If you are staying in someone's home, you may not want to disturb them by switching on a light - but it really is not worth the risk.

I do not want to stop you having fun, but be aware that any sort of adventure activities on land or water do pose some risk and many countries do not have high safety standards. Animal rides, such as on camels or elephants, can potentially be dangerous.

If you are venturing into the ocean for swimming, find out about the local hazards including water safety. We have beautiful beaches in Australia, but many tourists don't realise how easily they can drown in the surf or be dragged out by rips.

It is wonderful to see wildlife in different regions of the world, but always find out about the risks they pose. Monkeys, for instance, can be a big attraction in parts of Asia but you should avoid handling them because they can bite and may carry Rabies or other diseases.

A final word about safety

The key thing to remember is that by being safety and security conscious, and taking a few simple precautions, you can increase your chances of remaining healthy, preventing mishaps, and avoiding scams. That means you can focus on having a wonderful time!

My Top 7 Travel Photography Tips

Most of us love to record our travels by taking photographs, and they help to bring back many happy memories long after we have returned home. Photography can also be a fascinating hobby, and you can share images with friends on social media, write travel journals, or display them as a slideshow when entertaining.

Years ago, I would return from a trip with rolls of film that needed to be developed and printed, either by mail order or at a store. Now we have digital photography, and most small cameras are able to take excellent photos. We can choose to take as many photos as we like, knowing that we can quickly and easily delete those that aren't successful.

I used to return from a trip with thousands of photographs. Since then, I have modified my approach but still love to look back on my vacation snaps. Here are my top seven travel photography tips.

Tip 1: Choose the right camera for you

Serious photographers will purchase an SLR camera that can take high quality images, while many others use a compact camera or the camera in their smartphone or tablet device. Learn about all the features so that you can take advantage of them, but you can also choose to keep it simple and rely on the automatic settings. That is a reasonably foolproof way to take good images.

Enjoying your trip is the most important priority, so don't be too worried about taking photographs that are worthy of a prize. Remember to take some shots that include you and your friends or family – but you don't need to make every shot a selfie.

Tip 2: Don't take too many photos

There really is no need to take thousands of photographs and spend your vacation with a camera in front of your face. When you return home your friends and relatives will enjoy seeing a few of your travel shots but by the time you get to the thousandth one, their patience is guaranteed to be at an end. You will also face significant storage issues, and find that you rarely get time to look at all those images.

Take just a few well-chosen photos, and you will be able to review and enjoy them frequently when you return home. You will also have more fun on your vacation, freed from the responsibility of recording everything in sight.

I used to be almost like an addict, constantly clicking the camera in an effort to take a snap of everything I saw. A few years ago, I decided to cut back, go cold turkey, and restrict myself to capturing a small selection of the most interesting sights. I still return home with plenty of photos, but I am better able to see and experience everything on my journey.

Tip 3: Download your photos every night

Be sure to carry at least one spare battery for your camera and one or two memory cards. It is not fun to be far from your hotel room, standing in front of some new and amazing spectacle, and then discovering that your camera battery is flat.

I learned, the hard way, the virtue of downloading and saving my photos on a regular basis. About five years ago in Tangier, Morocco, a man ran past and grabbed my camera – along with all my wonderful vacation photographs. We had been on a long cruise and had visited some incredible places, such as Petra in Jordan, the Suez Canal, Athens and Pompeii.

Don't make the same mistake that I did. Be sure to download your images each night to keep them safe, and preferably also put them into some form of cloud storage. You can then charge the battery in your camera or device ready for the next day.

Tip 4: Compose your shots carefully

Choose the main points of interest in a shot and try to frame them carefully before you click the camera. Make sure the main features occupy most of the photo and try to have the major focus of interest slightly to the left of centre. You can, of course, be creative and try different sorts of arrangements.

Be sure to include some photos of yourself and your companions as well as local people. One of my favourite shots is of two women in Guatemala who are holding bags overflowing with their colourful embroidery. Make sure that anyone you photograph is framed well in the shot. My hubby once took a close-up of me and managed to cut my head off at the neck. Luckily, his photography skills have greatly improved since then.

Tip 5: Consider the lighting

Lighting is possibly the most important factor in taking a great photograph. Natural lighting always works best, which is convenient for travel photography as you will generally be taking outdoor shots. Soft and indirect lighting is ideal, while bright sunlight can be harsh and wash out colours and details.

You can't always control the lighting, especially as you may only be in a location for a short period time, perhaps in the middle of the day. Just remember to aim for soft, natural and indirect light whenever possible.

Tip 6: How to take videos

It is great to be able to take the occasional short video while on your travels, and most cameras now include that capability. Remember that videos use up more data than images, so make sure that you have the storage space for them.

If you are a beginning videographer, the first rule to follow is to keep your camera rock steady as you film any sort of activity. That produces a good, professional result, and prevents the effect of appearing to be in a magnitude 8 earthquake.

The second thing to learn is the technique for panning across a scene, such as a panorama. Once again, keep the camera steady and move it very slowly from one side to the other over several seconds.

The final simple technique is to avoid using the zoom feature on your videocamera. If you want to close in on something, then hold the camera steady and walk up to it. That gives you the zooming effect, but gives your video a much more professional look.

Tip 7: Be security conscious

I have already mentioned various aspects of safety in the previous chapter, but remember that it is easy to become distracted when you are focused on taking that once-in-a-lifetime shot of some extraordinary sight. That is the moment when you can be susceptible to a pickpocket. Always be aware of your surroundings and keep a firm hold of your belongings. Don't leave your handbag gaping open and never put it down on the ground.

Be wary of strangers who offer to take your photo, as there is a chance that they may run off with your camera. Instead of that, try asking another tourist or someone you know.

With all of those simple tips and tricks, you can have fun taking your vacation photos and they will bring back happy memories long after you return home.

My 7 Top Tips for Senior Travel

Senior travel has surged in popularity over the last twenty years, with many retired people taking overseas trips and exploring their own country - often for months at a time. In Australia they have become a significant sub-class that are fondly referred to as grey nomads.

If you have been hesitant about travelling overseas because of your age, then I urge you to have a look at the options that are available. There are ways to ensure that you have a comfortable and enjoyable journey from the time you leave home, and even tours designed exclusively for people over fifty. On the other hand, if you want to travel independently then you will find that it is not as challenging as you might imagine.

Here are my seven top tips for senior travel.

Tip 1: Consider your health and fitness

When planning a trip, you need to realistically assess your own physical limitations and health status, as that will impact the length and style of trip that you choose. It is no good signing up for a walking tour when you are about have a knee replacement, and you can't sign up for a three month cruise when you need medical treatment at your local hospital every six weeks.

It is essential to have travel insurance to cover you for any emergency medical expenses that might arise. Any pre-existing conditions that you have will need to be assessed by your insurer. You may have to pay a higher premium, but shop around for the best deal. If your application is denied then, unfortunately, that will prevent you from travelling.

Be sure to bring all your medications for the trip in your hand luggage, and check if any of those medications are restricted or banned in any country that you are planning to visit. If they are, find out how you can satisfy their requirements.

Travel usually involves some walking, and also long days that can be tiring. If you haven't been getting enough exercise then try taking a short walk each day in preparation for your trip. Your fitness levels will improve and you will be better able to see the sights and enjoy your vacation.

Tip 2: Time your travel to avoid crowds

Being retired means that you can travel at the best time of year to save money and avoid big crowds. If the peak season is summer, then that means you will also be avoiding hot weather. I enjoyed a Mediterranean cruise in winter, and found that there were no crowds or long lines anywhere, even in the centre of Rome. It was cold but the temperatures were not extreme, so it was ideal for walking.

However, you should steer clear of winter in regions where there is likely to be snow and ice. The severe weather may hinder your travels, with the possibility of transport delays due to fog or blizzards. It is also more hazardous for you to walk around, as it can be easy to slip over. You may also find many attractions closed for the winter, except in major cities.

Try to avoid school holidays by searching online to find the term times for local schools. Check also to find out if there are big local festivals, elections or special events such as international sporting competitions and conferences. While you might may have a long-held desire to see something like the Mardi Gras in Rio de Janeiro, less crowds will mean easier sightseeing and increased comfort and safety for you.

Tip 3: Senior discounts

Many travel companies and cruise lines offer discounts for seniors and also military discounts. There may be discounts available for admission to museums, galleries, and other attractions, and also on public transport. While these may sometimes be restricted to local citizens, some countries are extremely generous to seniors.

Wherever you go, always check the price list and ask if there is discount for seniors.

Be wary, however, of travel and tour prices that are advertised as being great value for seniors. Many of these are available to any other customer at the same price – or you may find a lower price for the same trip elsewhere.

Tip 4: Tour options suitable for seniors

Your budget, health and fitness are the main things that will limit your travel options. If you feel comfortable with travelling independently, you can create your own itinerary and take yourself almost anywhere in the world. If you want to be looked after as much as possible, you can choose a fully escorted tour, or a cruise, where everything is taken care of for you, including your luggage handling. While there are special tours designed only for seniors, you will find that many other escorted tours and cruises will have a significant cohort of older travellers, unless they are advertised as being for younger people.

Always read the find print in any escorted tour to make sure that it suitable for you. Some may involve more rigorous physical activity or include travel to more remote locations. On the other hand, there are camping expeditions designed with luxury in mind. You may prefer a tour that is designed to be leisurely, with stays of two or three nights in each location.

Try to give yourself some time to recover from a long flight before you embark on a tour, and allow plenty of time to get to an airport or make connections.

Tip 5: Cruises

Cruises are ideal for senior travel, unless you need to remain in close proximity to a hospital. Meals and entertainment are provided, and you are looked after from the time you board the ship until you disembark. When you visit ports, you can choose to do the shore excursions, explore the location independently or even stay on board and relax. Most cruise ships have a medical centre on board with a doctor.

While they come at a hefty price, you can select options that include flights, luggage handling and transfers from the ship to the airport. They can also organise accommodation before or after your cruise.

Unless you are a party animal, try to avoid the cruise lines that cater to younger people and families, and choose those that are favoured by more mature travellers. There are some elderly people who live full-time on cruise ships, claiming that it is less expensive than a nursing home and far more enjoyable.

Tip 6: Mobility issues

Having impaired mobility is no longer a barrier to travel, particularly in developed countries. Luggage transfers can be arranged, and many buildings have elevators or ramps. I have seen thousands of elderly people with all manner of physical limitations, with walking sticks, frames, wheelchairs and scooters, managing to get around and explore the world.

Be wary of travel to developing countries, where lack of facilities may be an issue for those with impaired mobility. In Asia, for instance, major attractions such as temples are often sited at the top of a tall staircase. Walking around can be precarious, as kerbs are often in poor condition.

Tip 7: Taking long trips

The wonderful thing about retirement is that you now have the time to travel. Why not consider taking an extended trip, or staying in some stunning location for a few months?

There are many longer cruises available, some lasting for months and taking you all around the world. You can settle into shipboard life, establish a daily routine, and enjoy the experience of being transported from one place to another while you relax onboard.

You may have a long-held dream to live overseas for a while, or stay in one location for a few months and explore the region from you home base. For instance, you could rent an apartment or villa in Italy or France, experience everyday life, take some cooking classes and practise the language skills that you were studying at home. You could also opt to take a longer tour or travel independently for an extended period of time. Having lived for a short period in both Washington D.C. and near London, I can tell you that there is nothing better than having the time to really get to know another place in depth.

Another option is to do an escorted tour and a cruise interspersed with some short stays and independent travel.

Bon Voyage

The big day has dawned and you are ready to walk out that front door and see the world. I hope that you have a safe and happy journey but before you leave here are five final things to check.

1. Do a last-minute security inspection of your house to be certain that all lights, heating and electrical or electronic devices are switched off. Throw out the trash, including any perishables still in your refrigerator.

2. Make sure that you have your entire luggage, including a folder with all tickets and vouchers, plus your wallet, glasses and medications.

3. Confirm that you have your passport and any visas.

4. Send a good-bye message to your closest family member and/or friends.

5. Make sure that all doors and windows are firmly secured.

At last, you are on your way!

THE END

A Note from the Author

Thank you so much for reading *Happy Travels 101*. If you enjoyed it, please tell your friends and spread the word on your favourite social media sites, including Facebook, Goodreads, Twitter and Pinterest.

Would you be able to take a moment to review this book on Amazon and share your opinion? That allows me to hear your views, and will also help other potential readers.

My Amazon Author page is an easy way to access my books, including The Jotham Fletcher Mystery Thriller Series.

Book 1: *The Magus Covenant*

Book 2: *The Rock of Magus*

Book 3: *The Magus Epiphany*

You can read more about me on my website at www.tonipike.com. I would be delighted to hear from you, and please let me know if you would like to be added to my email list.

If you'd like to see some of my travel photos, have a look at my Instagram page: @authorlovestravel.

Wishing you a lifetime of safe and happy travels,

Yours sincerely,

Toni Pike

51148156R00035

Made in the USA
Lexington, KY
31 August 2019